To Steve and Bill, with love—T.R.

.

The editors would like to thank
BARBARA KIEFER, Ph.D.,
Charlotte S. Huck Professor of Children's Literature,
The Ohio State University, and
MICHAEL W. YOGMAN, M.D., Department of Pediatrics at
Harvard Medical School, Boston,
for their assistance in the preparation of this book.

Visit us on the Web!
www.randomhouse.com/kids
Seussville.com

Educators and librarians, for a variety of teaching tools, visit us at
www.randomhouse.com/teachers

Library of Congress Cataloging-in-Publication Data
Rabe, Tish.
Inside your outside! / by Tish Rabe ; illustrated by Aristides Ruiz.
  p. cm. — (The Cat in the Hat's learning library)
Summary: The Cat in the Hat takes Sally and Dick on a trip in his Inside-Your-Outside
Machine.
ISBN 978-0-375-81100-5 (trade) — ISBN 978-0-375-91100-2 (lib. bdg.)
1. Human anatomy—Juvenile literature. [1. Human anatomy. 2. Body, Human.]
I. Ruiz, Aristides, ill. II. Title. III. Series.
QM27 .R33 2003 611—dc21 2002013431

Printed in the United States of America
27 26 25 24

Inside Your Outside!

by Tish Rabe

illustrated by Aristides Ruiz

The Cat in the Hat's Learning Library®

Random House 🏠 New York

I'm the Cat in the Hat
here to share some good news.
From the tips of your hair
to the toes in your shoes . . .

6

your body is moving.

It never stops going.

Right now your heart's beating.

Right now your blood's flowing.

You may be just sitting

and reading a book,

but your body is busy.

Come on, take a look!

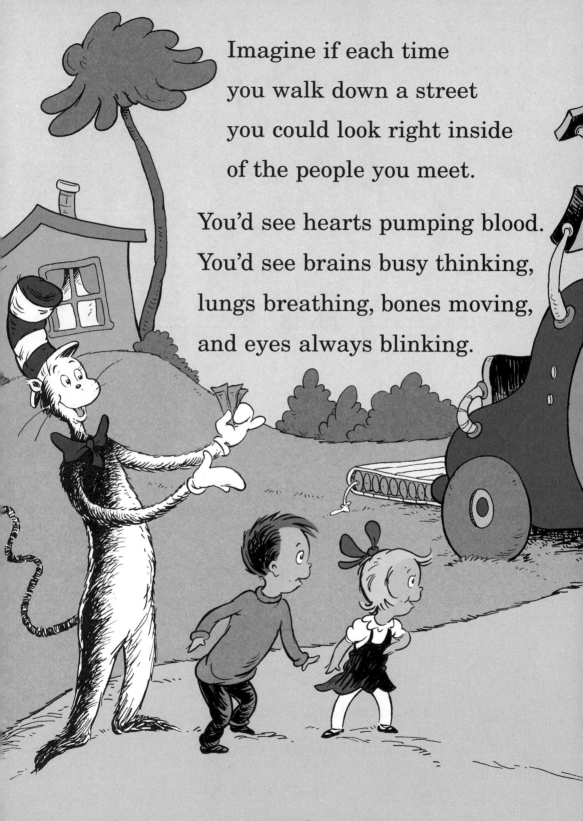

Imagine if each time
you walk down a street
you could look right inside
of the people you meet.

You'd see hearts pumping blood.
You'd see brains busy thinking,
lungs breathing, bones moving,
and eyes always blinking.

There's one easy way
you can see what I mean.
Take a ride in my
Inside-Your-Outside Machine.

in
inside-your-
Outside
Machine

Every ticket is free and
before we are through,
you will see inside me
and inside of you, too!

9

Let's start at the top with
your brain. It is key.
It controls all you do—
helps you laugh, learn, and see.

It makes your legs move
when you run, jump, or walk.
It makes your face move
when you blink, smile, and talk.

It sends information
to all parts of you
and does millions of things
no computer can do!

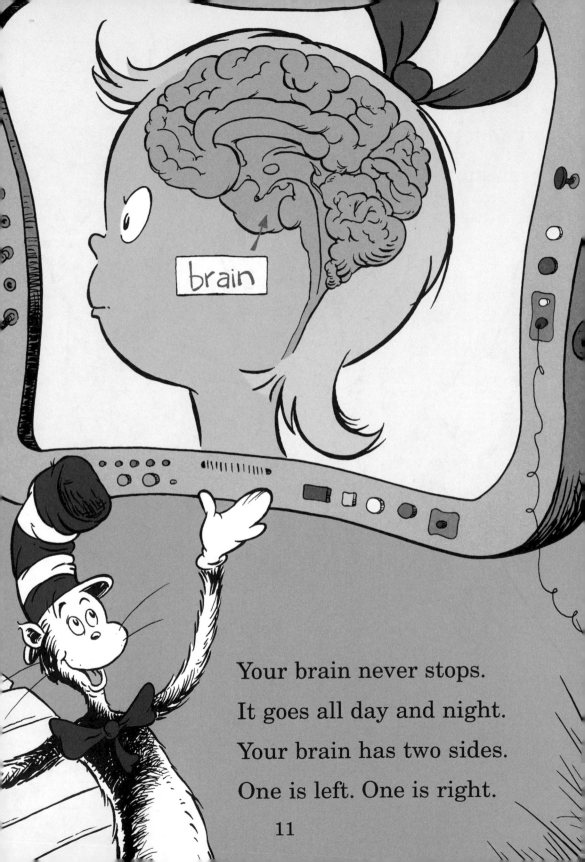

brain

Your brain never stops.
It goes all day and night.
Your brain has two sides.
One is left. One is right.

11

Different things are controlled
by each side of your brain.
The left helps you read and
remember my name.

left brain

cat

Meet the Feletons, who
live in far-off Fadin.
When they stand in the sun,
you can see through their skin!

It is easy to see (when
you look at a Feleton)
all of the bones that are
known as a skeleton.

Bones shape our bodies
and help us stand tall.
We've two hundred and six.
Some are big. Some are small.

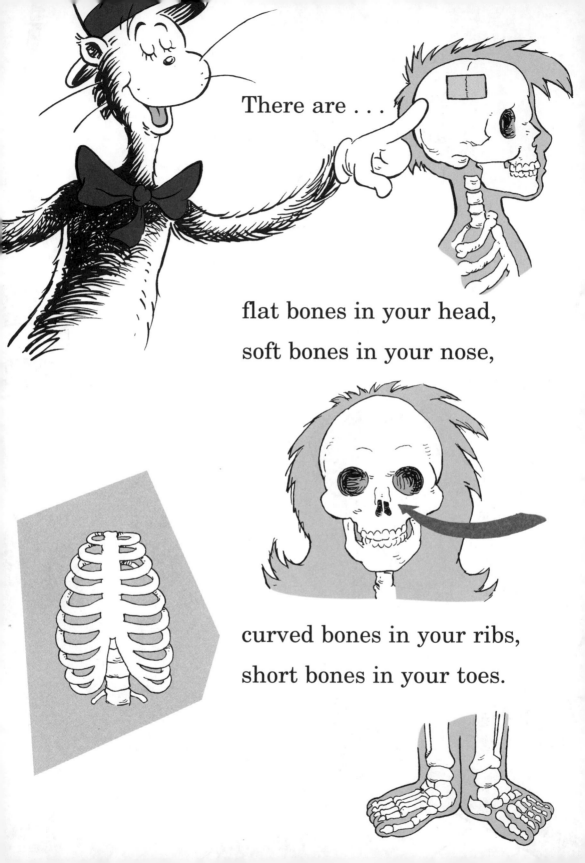

There are . . .

flat bones in your head,
soft bones in your nose,

curved bones in your ribs,
short bones in your toes.

One bone in your ear
(this made us think twice)
is so small—it's the size
of just one grain of rice!

ear bone

rice

Bones in your body
are stronger than steel,
but when a bone breaks,
it is able to heal.

elbow joint

wrist joint

Here is a fact that we
both think is neat.
A joint is the place where
two different bones meet.

There are bones down your back
that are all in a line.
They help you stand up and
are known as the spine.

The spine has a spinal cord
running inside it—
a bundle of nerves which help
move it and guide it.

Here is a word that
we just learned today.
The bones in your spine
are called vert-e-brae.

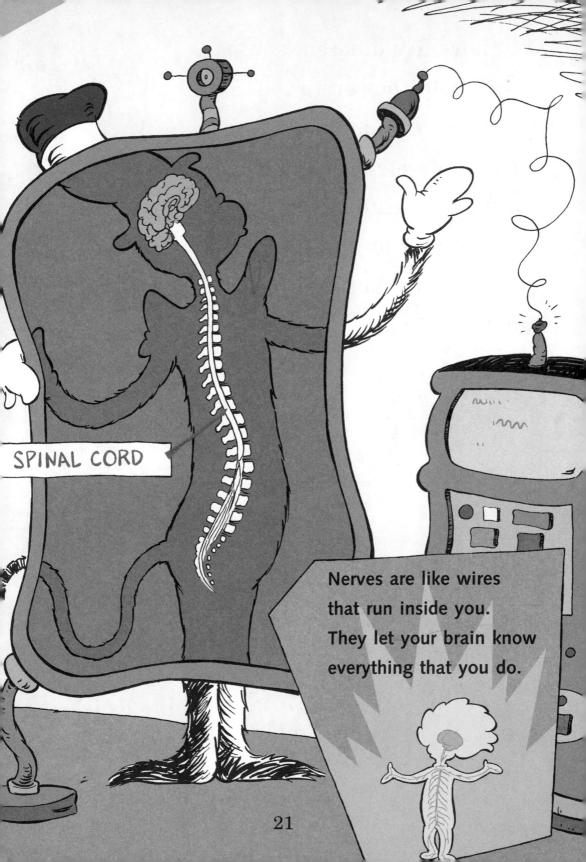

SPINAL CORD

Nerves are like wires
that run inside you.
They let your brain know
everything that you do.

You have five different senses
which help your brain tell
what you hear, how things taste,
what you see, touch, and smell.
Sniff a flower and pull
sweet smells to your nose.
Nerves go to your brain and
say, "Hey! That's a rose!"

Your sense of touch
really tells you a lot.
This kitten is soft.
This pizza is HOT!

taste

touch

sight

If you could not see,
other senses, it's true,
like touch, taste, and smell,
would work harder for you.

Sound waves travel through air
deep into your ear,
shaking your eardrum.
That is how you can hear.

ear anatomy

Anvil

Stirrup

Hammer

Cochlea

Eardrum

Why do you feel dizzy when you have stopped twirling? Inside of your ears there is liquid still swirling.

Your poor dizzy brain just has no way of knowing whether you've stopped or if you're still going.

taste

Bitter
Sour
Salty
Sweet

Pickles

THING 2

Taste buds on your tongue
tell your brain when you eat—
"This pickle is sour!"
"This ice cream is sweet!"

When your eye looks at something,
it goes to your brain,
and there something happens
that's hard to explain.

Sight

Iris

Nerve to Brai

Lens

Cornea

Pupil

Retina

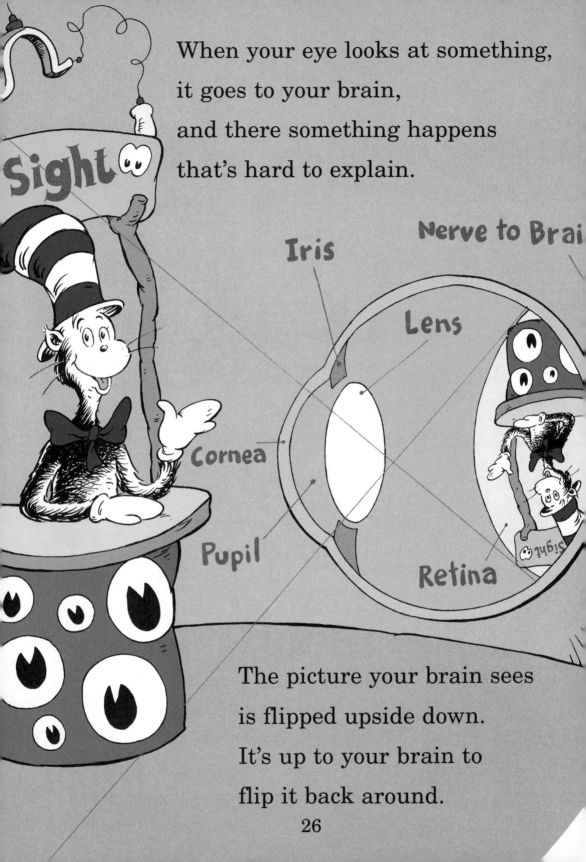

The picture your brain sees
is flipped upside down.
It's up to your brain to
flip it back around.

26

Nearsighted folks can see
things that are near,
but faraway things
do not look quite as clear.

Farsighted folks can see
things that are far,
but things that are close:
My, how blurry they are!

I'm farsighted.
He's nearsighted.
But we agree—
with our glasses we see
far and near easily.

When you move, muscles pull
on your bones and help you
turn your head, raise your hand,
take a bite, and then chew.

Some muscles are joined
to each other or skin.
They help wiggle your ears,
raise your eyebrows, and grin.

Muscles

Here's a fact about muscles
we've known for a while.
You use more when you frown
than you use when you smile.

You have six hundred muscles
and here's the best part.
The biggest of all is
your very own heart!

The sound that your chest makes
is "thump—thump—thump—thump."
That's the sound of your blood
being moved by a pump.

The pump is your heart.
Blood flows through it and then
the heart muscle squeezes
the blood out again.

Blood circles your body
in less than a minute.

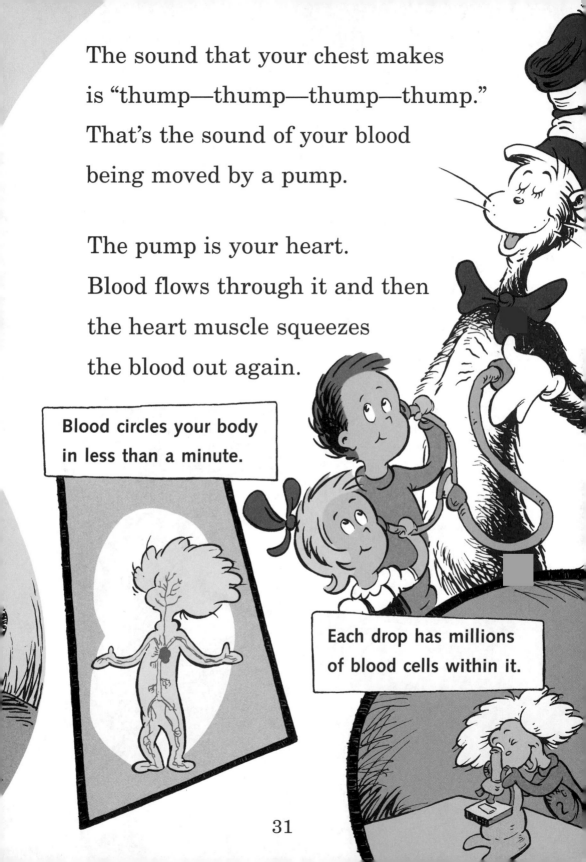

Each drop has millions
of blood cells within it.

Blood cells are two colors.
There are red cells and white.
If a germ makes you sick,
that germ's in for a fight.

A white blood cell gets ready
the minute it meets it.
It wraps up that germ,
then the white blood cell eats it!

Red cells give blood color.
Look closely—you'll see.
They look just like doughnuts
without holes to me!

BLOOD TANK

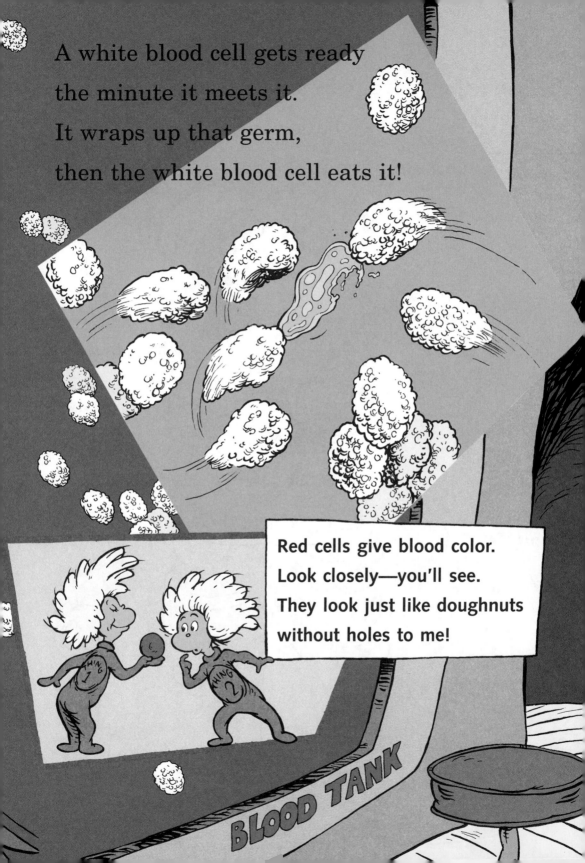

Lungs help you to breathe
and they never can rest.
They're like two balloons
in each side of your chest.

Inhale: breathe
air in.

Every four seconds you
breathe in and out.
Lungs bring in air, which
you can't live without.

Exhale: let
air out.

Each time that you eat,
the first thing that you do
is put food in your mouth
and that's when you chew.

stomach

liver

large intestine

small intestine

Food goes into your stomach
(where juices are flowing),
turns into a paste—then
the paste keeps on going.

A tube—the intestine—
is what food moves through.
This food feeds your blood,
which then feeds all of you.

Food takes time to travel.
Thing One and I know
in our stomachs there's food
we ate three days ago!

When you drink, liquid
enters your blood and then goes
all over your body
wherever blood flows.

Blood is cleaned by your kidneys.
They work with great speed
to clean out waste and water
that you do not need.

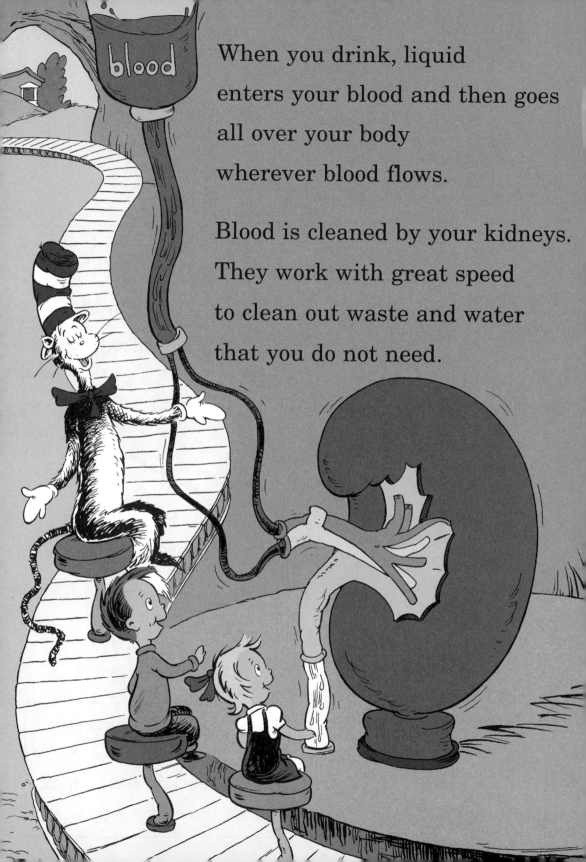

Waste water is stored
in your bladder and then
it soon flows back OUT of
your body again.

Restroom

You need food and water.
You use quite a bit of it.
If some is left over?
Your body gets rid of it!

We have come to the end
of our ride, it is true,
but there still is a lot
you can learn about you.

Way down deep inside
of your body and mine,
there's a lot going on
every day, all the time.

As you grow, you will know
that your bones will get longer,
your lungs will get bigger,
your muscles grow stronger.

Your brain and your heart
will guide all that you do.
Someone special is
inside your outside—it's . . .

YOU!

GLOSSARY

Blood: A bright red liquid that is pumped by the heart and carries food and oxygen to the body.

Eardrum: A thin tissue stretched like the top of a drum inside the ear.

Germ: A tiny particle that can cause disease.

Heal: To make healthy or sound again.

Information: Knowledge or facts about something.

Intestine: A long tube that goes down from the stomach and is divided into two parts— the small intestine and the large intestine.

Muscle: Tissue in the body made of strong fibers that tighten or relax to make the body move.

Pump: A machine that moves water or other liquids from one place to another.

Sound waves: Rapid movements through the air that are received by the ear.

FOR FURTHER READING

Bones by Stephen Krensky, illustrated by Davy ones (Random House, *Step into Reading,* Step 2). earn about the skeleton inside you! For reschoolers and up.

Human Body by Steve Parker and Deni Bown Dorling Kindersley, *Eyewitness Explorers*). Photos nd illustrations show the many parts and functions f the human body. For kindergarten and up.

The Human Body, created by Gallimard Jeunesse Scholastic, *A First Discovery Book*). An introduction o the human body. For preschoolers and up.

Me and My Amazing Body by Joan Sweeney, llustrated by Annette Cable (Crown, Dragonfly). All bout your body! For preschoolers and up.

Why Don't Haircuts Hurt? Questions and Answers bout the Human Body by Melvin and Gilda Berger, llustrated by Karen Barnes (Scholastic). Find out he answers to lots of questions in this fact-filled ook about the human body. For grades 1 and up.

INDEX